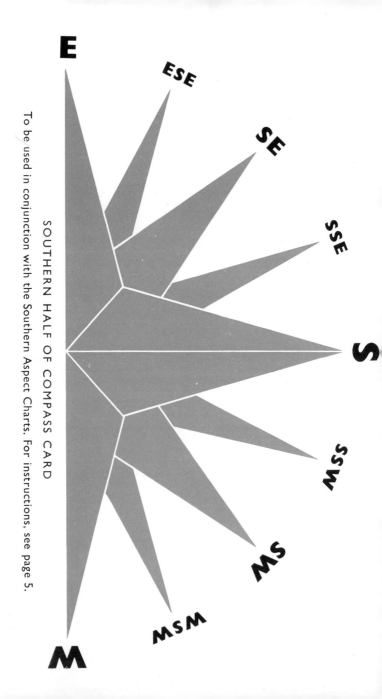

SOUTHERN HALF OF COMPASS CARD

To be used in conjunction with the Southern Aspect Charts. For instructions, see page 5.

# PHILIP'S

# STAR
# FINDER

● A month-by-month guide to the heavens ●

First published in 1918 as *Stars at a Glance*

Completely revised © 1959 and 1970

Retitled *Star Finder* 1991

© George Philip Ltd, 1991

George Philip Ltd, 59 Grosvenor Street, London, W1X 9DA

Printed in Hong Kong

## Contents

# Introduction to the study of the stars

Two facts are at once evident to a careful observer of the night-sky: (1) That the position of the stars is fixed relative to one another, and (2) that they appear to rotate round a central point near the star Polaris. This star is nearly overhead at the North Pole and in relation to it all other stars appear to follow parallel paths in a series of concentric circles called parallels of Declination.

## Apparent Rotation of the Stars

From the British Isles Polaris always appears due north, midway between the zenith which is directly overhead, and the northern horizon. From the British Isles, therefore, the parallel paths followed by the stars round Polaris are inclined at an angle to our horizon, the angle always being equal to the latitude of the observer. It follows that stars which are always low on the horizon at the North Pole appear to us to rise on our eastern horizon. After rising they ascend in the sky until they cross the southern meridian, and then descend until they set on the western horizon and finally disappear for the remainder of the journey along their circular pathway, until they re-emerge the following night. Because of this tilt many more stars are visible in Great Britain than at the North Pole, but, again for the same reason, not all at the same time. In their rotation about the Pole star certain of them never pass below the horizon and are known as Northern Circumpolar stars (see page 9). On the contrary, the Southern Circumpolar stars, being always below our horizon, are never visible to us (see page 40). Both by night and day the stars are pursuing their steady course overhead, though in daylight they are unseen because of the brilliance of the sun.

A complete rotation of the stars occupies 23 hours 56 minutes, the length of sidereal day, as opposed to the solar day of 24 hours. A star will therefore be seen in the same position in the night-sky four minutes earlier each succeeding night, or about two hours earlier every month. The effect of this is illustrated quite clearly by following the change in position of any constellation on the Monthly Aspect Charts. For example, follow the path of Orion on the Southern Aspect Charts, from October to March. This gain of four minutes a day on solar time results in an advance of about 24 hours in the year. Thus, any constellation returns to its original starting point in a year of 365 days, after making a complete revolution. It should be noted that in addition to showing the aspect of the stars for every month of the year, the charts also illustrate their aspect for every two hours of the night.

## Magnitude

Stars are classified into magnitudes according to their apparent brightness; that is, the amount of light apparently emitted. This qualification is important because a faint star may appear to be emitting less light than another merely because it is so much more distant. First magnitude stars are the most brilliant, and are two and a half times brighter than second magnitude stars, which in turn are two and a half times brighter than third magnitude stars, and so on. Magnitudes are shown by symbol on the charts. Recognition by magnitude is not very satisfactory, since the seasonable position of any one star may be the reason for considerable dimming due to the additional atmosphere through which it is viewed. Moreover, there may be local haze due to weather. The so-called variable stars appear to change their brilliancy and are represented on the charts by their average magnitude. They are of more interest to the regular than to the casual observer.

## The Milky Way

The Milky Way (omitted from the charts for the sake of greater clarity) is an indistinct luminous band stretching right across the heavens, and is formed by the concentrated light of countless stars that lie between us and the outer rim of the galaxy which is our universe. Under first-class conditions it is a striking phenomenon and is a useful aid in recognising groups which lie on or near to it.

## Constellations

Ancient astronomers arbitrarily separated the stars into groups, now known as constellations, and each group was conceived to represent some mythological figure and was named accordingly. The principal constellations are described on pages 41–48. The stars forming a constellation are rarely together in fact, but only appear so in our line of sight. Those of The Plough are an exception to this rule. Clusters, however, are compact groups travelling together, and are indicated on the charts by special symbols. Nebulæ are of several kinds, under the two main groupings of gaseous nebulæ—cloudy masses of luminous gas—and extra-galactic nebulæ, which are thought to be complete island universes so distant that the separate stars composing them are indistinguishable.

## Planets

Planets are satellites of the sun, and could almost be described as other earths, depending on the sun for heat, and shining by reason of its reflected light. They revolve in regular and clearly defined orbits round the sun, but, relative to the fixed stars, their motion is irregular and so it is not possible to show them on the charts. Their steady radiance is readily distinguished from the "twinkle" of the stars.

In addition to the notes on page 11, the reader is referred to Whitaker's Almanac, The Air Almanac, or some Nautical or Astronomical Almanac for the dates and times of the appearance of the planets. Mercury and Venus are nearer the Sun than the Earth is, and therefore only appear as morning or evening stars. Venus is the next brightest object in our heavens after the Sun and Moon. The sun, moon and planets all follow paths across the sky within a definite zone which has been named the Zodiac, and the Zodiacal constellations are those lying within this zone. The path of the sun is called the Ecliptic and is in the middle of this zone. Owing to the tilt of the Earth's axis the Ecliptic crosses the Equator at two points, known as the Spring and Autumn Equinoxes (see pages 17 and 29).

## Mapping the Stars

Although the distances of the stars from the Earth vary enormously, to us they appear to be on the inside of an enormous sphere enclosing the Earth. Mapping them offers the same problem of projection as mapping the Earth: that of representing a sphere, in this case the apparent sphere of the heavens, on the flat surface of a map. In mapping the celestial sphere, North and South Poles are considered to be directly above the North and South Poles of the Earth. This same principle also governs the position of the celestial equator or Equinoctial. Parallels of Latitude, however, become parallels of Declination, and meridians of Longitude are called Hour Circles of Right Ascension, usually abbreviated to "Decl." and "RA." The Sidereal Hour Angle (S.H.A.) has been adopted by the Royal Air Force, and it is represented by 360°—R.A. measured from the "First Point of Aries," i.e. the point where the Ecliptic intersects the Equinoctial on March 21st each year.

In preparing a flat copy of what is apparently a sphere it is impossible to avoid distortion at the edges of the chart. It has been kept to a minimum in this book by giving charts of the North and South on a Polar projection (pages 9 and 40) and the middle heavens (that part directly over the Equator) on a Mercator projection (pages 36–39). Any distortion is thus kept to the edges of the charts. All the stars which are included in the Planisphere Chart on pages 10 and 11 can be seen at some time from the British Isles.

## Aspect Charts

The Aspect Charts are drawn on a system peculiar to this book intended to simplify recognition. The lines indicate direction only, and do not in any way correspond with Declination and Right Ascension.

Although each double-page Aspect Chart forms a complete circle, it must be clearly understood that it comprises two semi-circular pictures of the heavens—one looking North and one looking South —and the bottom of each picture is that edge next to the binding. The zenith for the British Isles falls midway along the curved edge of each chart. From it lines are drawn to the points of the compass on the horizon. Thus the whole of the sky visible at the time for which the chart is drawn is divided into imaginary sectors. When comparing the chart with the sky, corresponding lines can be imagined in the sky which will serve as guide lines in identifying stars.

## Compass Cards

Just inside the covers of the book is a boldly designed compass card, the Southern portion at the front and the Northern portion at the back, which is clear enough to be read in dim light. The quarter points on it correspond with the lines on the Aspect Charts. By holding the unwanted pages vertically between the thumb and fore-finger so that the edge is toward the observer, it is easy to arrange that any Aspect Chart can be viewed at the same time as its appropriate half of the compass card. If at first the observer always uses the Northern chart and compass card, and fixes his position by Polaris, he can afterwards face the reverse direction and use the Southern chart and compass card. After the first few observations it will be possible to identify the constellations visible with little preliminary orientation.

Only the chief groups are given on the Aspect Charts, together with their popular English names. Once they have become familiar the less conspicuous groups may be sought, and instructions to that end are included in the catalogue of stars on pages 41–48, which can be used in conjunction with the more detailed plates on pages 9 and 36–39.

## Finding and naming stars without a compass

The simplest and most reliable guide to the true north direction is the **Pole Star (Polaris)**. An observer looking towards this star faces N., has his back to the S., and by extending his arms in line with the shoulders, obtains approximately W. and E. bearings. The relative positions and appearance of the following circumpolar guide-stars should be memorized by means of the Chart on page 9.

(i) **Dubhe** and **Merak**, "the Pointers" (Plough), are in a straight line with the Pole. The **Pole Star** lies a little to one side of this line.

(ii) **Caph** (Cassiopeia) and **Megrez** (Plough). The North Celestial Pole is at the centre of a straight line joining these stars.

(iii) **Vega** (Lyra) and **Capella** (Auriga) lie at a considerable distance on either side of the pole, almost at right angles. **Polaris** appears to lie about half way along a slightly-curved line between them.

*The first is the best method of finding the North Star, since the Plough cannot be mistaken, and it is always high enough on the sky to be easily seen above trees in uneven country, &c.*

When the N. is found the remaining points can be fairly accurately obtained by means of the compass card provided inside the covers of the book. Hold the Northern Half so that the point N. is directly under the **Pole Star.** The card is then a true compass, and the bearings from N. to E. and W. can be read off. Points at the horizon bearing due E. and W. should be noted, and the base of the Southern Half of the card aligned with them. It can then be used in the same way as the Northern Half, the observer now facing S. The two portions of the card are so arranged as to be easily used in conjunction with the North and South Aspect Charts respectively.

To identify a Star or Constellation visible at a given time:—

(i) With the aid of the Calendar-Index (page 7) select the Aspect Chart appropriate to the time and date of observation.

(ii) Imagine a *straight* line extending from the Zenith, through the Star, and by means of the Compass Card and **Pole Star** take the bearing of the point where the line reaches the horizon.

(iii) Find on the Aspect Chart the nearest bearing and guide-line (here *curved*), when the bright stars and groups near the imaginary line on the sky can be identified.

To find a certain star on the sky:—

(i) Find the star on the Aspect Chart for the time of observation, and note which of the guide-lines it is nearest.

(ii) Take the bearing of this line at the Horizon with the aid of the Compass Card and **Pole Star**, and imagine a straight line joining it to the Zenith.

(iii) Read off the most conspicuous stars near this line from the Chart, identifying the one required by its elevation or position in regard to other stars.

**Calendar Index** to the Monthly Aspect Charts (pp. 12–35)

Each pair of charts shows the principal stars visible between 9 p.m. and midnight during the month. To ascertain the appropriate charts for a particular time and date, find the time at the head of the diagram and follow the vertical column downwards to a point opposite to the required date. The diagonal band in which this point lies will indicate the charts to be consulted.

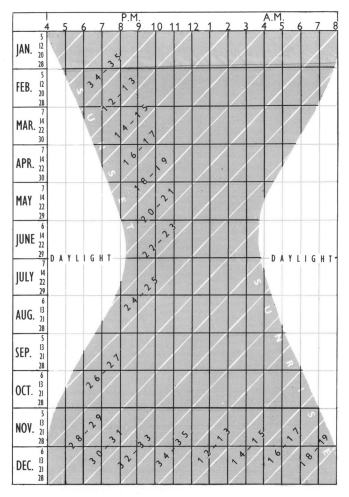

# Air Navigation Stars

The following fifty-seven stars appear in the Air Almanac. The list comprises three groups, the first one of twenty-two stars being most important. Mention should also be made of Polaris (mag. 2.1—Ursa Minor), a very important star for navigators.

| Name | Mag. | Constellation | Name | Mag. | Constellation |
|---|---|---|---|---|---|
| Achernar | 0.6 | Eridanus | Dubhe | 1.9 | Ursa Major |
| Acrux | 1.0 | Crux Australis | Fomalhaut | 1.3 | Piscis Austr. |
| Aldebaran | 1.1 | Taurus | Peacock | 2.1 | Pavo |
| Alpheratz | 2.1 | Andromeda | Pollux | 1.2 | Gemini |
| Altair | 0.9 | Aquila | Procyon | 0.5 | Canis Minor |
| Antares | 1.2 | Scorpius | Regulus | 1.3 | Leo |
| Arcturus | 0.2 | Boötes | Rigel | 0.3 | Orion |
| Betelgeuse | | | Rigil Kent | 0.1 | Centaurus |
| | 0.1 to 1.2 | Orion | Sirius | —1.6 | Canis Major |
| Canopus | —0.9 | Argo Navis | Spica | 1.2 | Virgo |
| Capella | 0.2 | Auriga | Vega | 0.1 | Lyra |
| Deneb | 1.3 | Cygnus | | | |
| | | | | | |
| Alioth | 1.7 | Ursa Major | Kochab | 2.2 | Ursa Minor |
| Alkaid | 1.9 | Ursa Major | Nunki | 2.1 | Sagittarius |
| Alphard | 2.2 | Hydra | Rasalhague | 2.1 | Ophiuchius |
| Denebola | 2.2 | Leo | Schedar | 2.5 | Cassiopeia |
| Diphda | 2.2 | Cetus | Shaula | 1.7 | Scorpius |
| Hamal | 2.2 | Aries | Suhail | 2.2 | Argo Navis |
| | | | | | |
| Acamar | 3.1 | Eridanus | | | |
| Adhara | 1.6 | Canis Major | Gacrux | 1.6 | Crux Austr. |
| Al Na'ir | 2.2 | Grus | Gienah | 2.8 | Pegasus |
| Alnilam | 1.8 | Orion | Hadar | 0.9 | Centaurus |
| Alphecca | 2.3 | CoronaBorealis | Kaus Austr. | 2.0 | Sagittarius |
| Ankaa | 2.4 | Phoenix | Markab | 2.6 | Pegasus |
| Atria | 1.9 | Triang. Austr. | Menkar | 2.8 | Cetus |
| Avior | 1.7 | Argo Navis | Menkent | 2.3 | Centaurus |
| Bellatrix | 1.7 | Orion | Miaplacidus | 1.8 | Argo Navis |
| Elnath | 1.8 | Taurus | Mirfak | 1.9 | Perseus |
| Eltanin | 2.4 | Draco | Sabik | 2.6 | Ophiuchius |
| Enif | 2.5 | Pegasus | Zuben'ubi | 2.9 | Libra |

Reference to many of these stars is made in the section at the end of this book describing the constellations and giving hints on their location and other interesting facts.

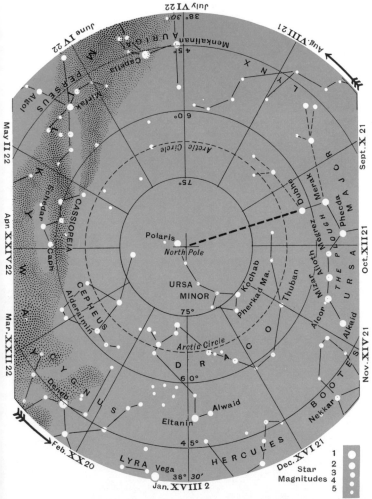

The Stars shown above are (theoretically) *always visible* from or north of the latitude of London. The direction of their apparent revolution is indicated by arrows. The dates correspond with those of the Aspect Charts (Plates 12–35) and show when the R.A. circles touch the north point of the horizon at 10 p.m., the distance between them representing two hours' motion.

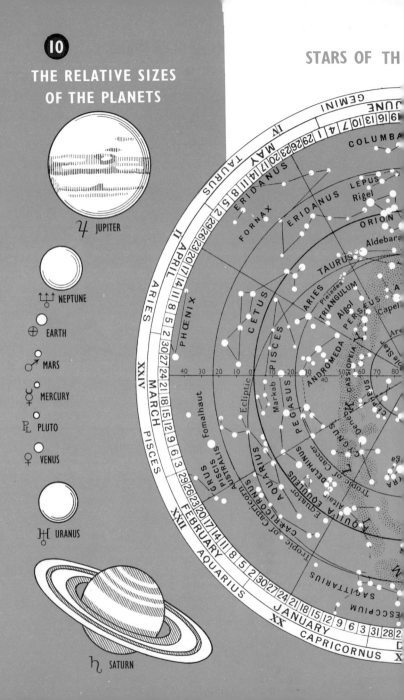

**10**

## THE RELATIVE SIZES
## OF THE PLANETS

♃ JUPITER

♅♁ NEPTUNE

⊕ EARTH

♂ MARS

☿ MERCURY

♇ PLUTO

♀ VENUS

♅ URANUS

♄ SATURN

GEMINI

JUNE

COLUMBA

LEPUS

Rigel

ORION

Aldebara

ERIDANUS

ERIDANUS

FORNAX

TAURUS

MAY

TAURUS

APRIL

PHOENIX

ARIES

PISCES

CETUS

ARIES

Pleiades

TRIANGULUM

Algol

PERSEUS

Capel

ANDROMEDA

CASSIOPEIA

40 30 20 10 0 -10 -20 -30 40 50 60 70 80

Ecliptic

Markab

PEGASUS

CEPHEUS

MARCH

XXIV

Fomalhaut

PISCIS

AUSTRALIS

GRUS

Deneb

CYGNUS

DELPHINUS

AQUILA

EQUULEUS

Altair

Equator

Tropic of Capricorn

AQUARIUS

CAPRICORNUS

FEBRUARY

XXII

PISCES

AQUARIUS

JANUARY

XX

CAPRICORNUS

SAGITTARIUS

SCORPIUM

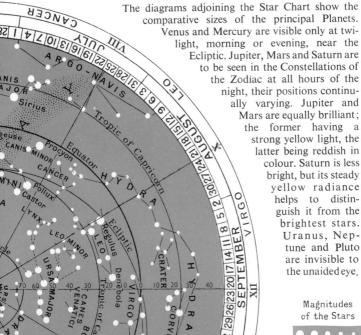

The diagrams adjoining the Star Chart show the comparative sizes of the principal Planets. Venus and Mercury are visible only at twilight, morning or evening, near the Ecliptic. Jupiter, Mars and Saturn are to be seen in the Constellations of the Zodiac at all hours of the night, their positions continually varying. Jupiter and Mars are equally brilliant; the former having a strong yellow light, the latter being reddish in colour. Saturn is less bright, but its steady yellow radiance helps to distinguish it from the brightest stars. Uranus, Neptune and Pluto are invisible to the unaided eye.

Magnitudes
of the Stars

1   2   3   4   5

The Chart shows the principal Fixed Stars visible from the British Isles. The actual portions of the Heavens visible at any date can be seen on the Aspect Charts. The twelve Right Ascension Hour Circles here shown form the middle lines of the Northern Aspect Charts for midnight of the dates which they subtend at the margin of this Chart. For the Northern Heavens in greater detail see plates 9, 36–37, 38–39.

*Capricornus*

♑

The principal January Stars are shown here and on the opposite page. Their positions are correct for January 5th at 11 p.m. and January 20th at 10 p.m., and for four minutes earlier on each succeeding night, e.g. Jan 1st at 11.16 p.m., 6th at 10.56 p.m., 21st at 9.56 p.m., &c.

This aspect of the heavens is also correct for December 21st at midnight; Feb. 5th at 9 p.m.; 20th at 8 p.m.; March 7th at 7 p.m.

The Stars move from the positions here shown to those on the next pair of Aspect Charts in the space of two hours.

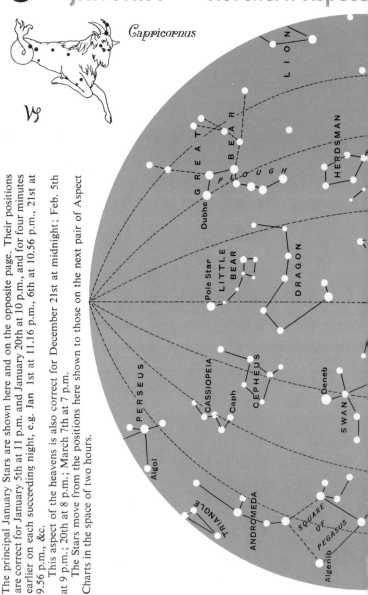

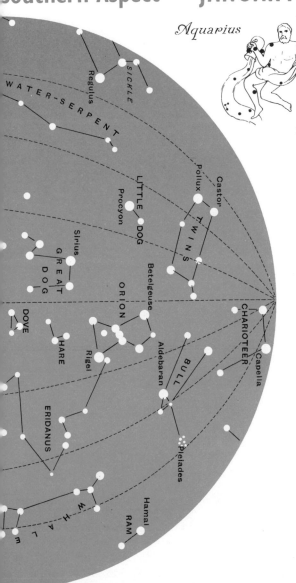

*Aquarius*

At the beginning of January the Sun is in the sign of Capricornus, but passes into Aquarius about the end of the third week. On January 1st, day breaks at 6h 2m and sunrise is at 8h 8m a.m.; the Sun sets at 4h and twilight ends at 6h 4m p.m., the length of actual daylight being about 7 hours 50 minutes. During the month the mornings increase by 25 minutes and the afternoons by 45 minutes.

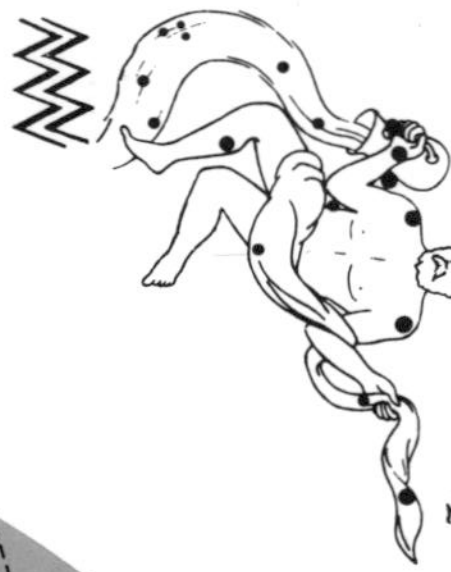

*Aquarius*

The principal February Stars are shown here and on the opposite page. Their positions are correct for February 5th at 11 p.m. and February 20th at 10 p.m., and for four minutes earlier on each succeeding night, e.g. Feb. 1st at 11.16 p.m., 6th at 10.56 p.m., 21st at 9.56 p.m., &c.

This aspect of the heavens is also correct for January 20th at midnight; March 7th at 9 p.m.; 22nd at 8 p.m.

The Stars move from the positions here shown to those on the next pair of Aspect Charts in the space of two hours.

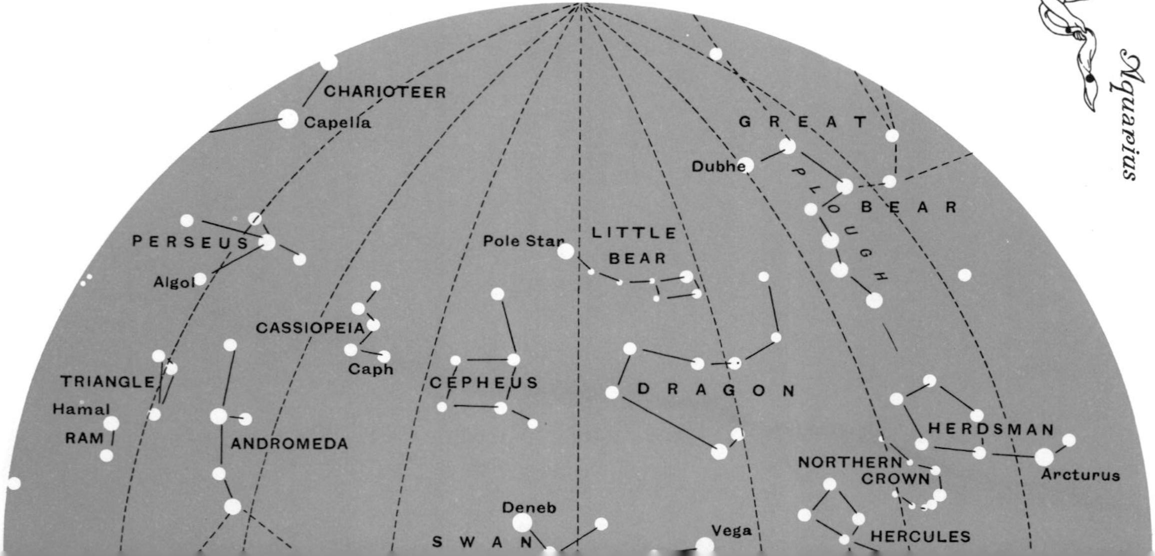

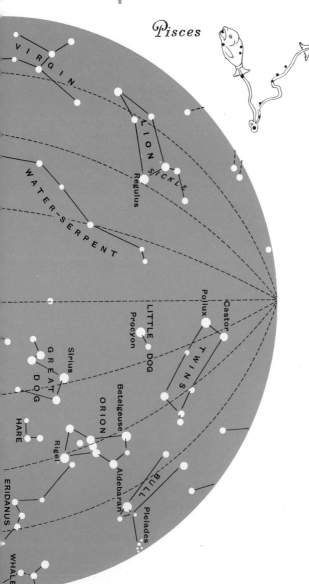

*Pisces*

H

At the beginning of February the Sun is in the sign of Aquarius, and passes into Pisces after the middle of the month. On February 1st, day breaks at 5h 50m and sunrise is at 7h 42m a.m. The Sun sets at 4h 45m and twilight ends at 6h 45m, the length of actual daylight being about 9 hours.

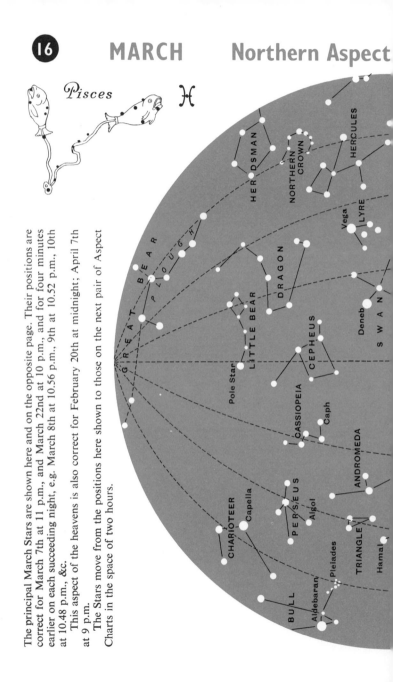

*Pisces* ♓

The principal March Stars are shown here and on the opposite page. Their positions are correct for March 7th at 11 p.m., and March 22nd at 10 p.m., and for four minutes earlier on each succeeding night, e.g. March 8th at 10.56 p.m., 9th at 10.52 p.m., 10th at 10.48 p.m., &c.

This aspect of the heavens is also correct for February 20th at midnight; April 7th at 9 p.m.

The Stars move from the positions here shown to those on the next pair of Aspect Charts in the space of two hours.

HERDSMAN

NORTHERN CROWN

HERCULES

LYRE

Vega

G R E A T   B E A R

P L O U G H

DRAGON

LITTLE BEAR

Deneb

S W A N

CEPHEUS

Pole Star

CASSIOPEIA

Caph

ANDROMEDA

CHARIOTEER

Capella

PERSEUS

Algol

TRIANGLE

Hamal

BULL

Aldebaran

Pleiades

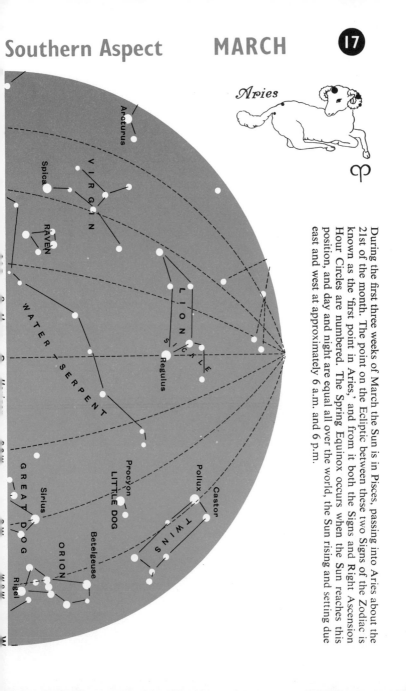

*Aries*

During the first three weeks of March the Sun is in Pisces, passing into Aries about the 21st of the month. The point on the Ecliptic between these two Signs of the Zodiac is known as the 'first point in Aries,' and from it both the Signs and Right Ascension Hour Circles are numbered. The Spring Equinox occurs when the Sun reaches this position, and day and night are equal all over the world, the Sun rising and setting due east and west at approximately 6 a.m. and 6 p.m.

Arcturus

Spica

VIRGIN

RAVEN

LION

SICKLE

Regulus

WATER

SERPENT

Procyon

LITTLE DOG

Pollux

Castor

TWINS

GREAT

Sirius

DOG

ORION

Betelgeuse

Rigel

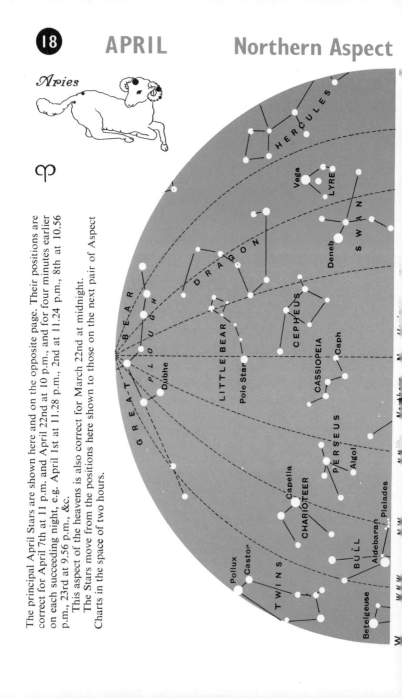

*Aries*

♈

The principal April Stars are shown here and on the opposite page. Their positions are correct for April 7th at 11 p.m. and April 22nd at 10 p.m., and for four minutes earlier on each succeeding night, e.g. April 1st at 11.28 p.m., 2nd at 11.24 p.m., 8th at 10.56 p.m., 23rd at 9.56 p.m., &c.

This aspect of the heavens is also correct for March 22nd at midnight.

The Stars move from the positions here shown to those on the next pair of Aspect Charts in the space of two hours.

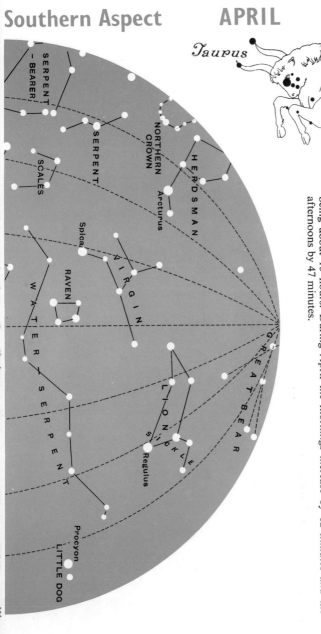

*Taurus*

♉

The Sun is in Aries until about April 22nd, when it passes into the sign Taurus. Days are now longer than nights. On April 1st day breaks at 3h 35m and sunrise is at 5h 38m a.m. The Sun sets at 6h 30m and twilight ends at 8h 30m p.m., the period of actual daylight being about 13 hours. During April the mornings increase by 62 minutes and the afternoons by 47 minutes.

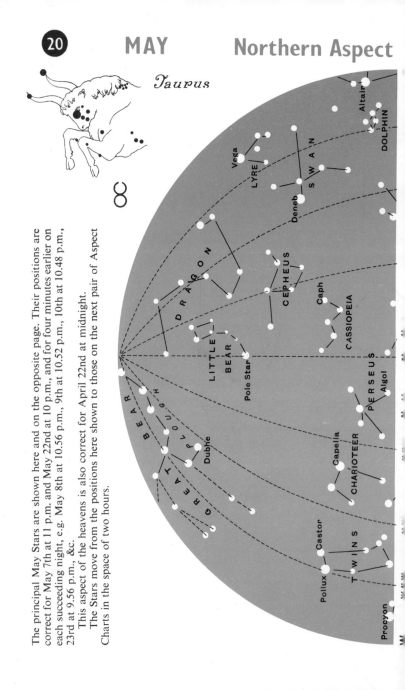

*Taurus*

♉

The principal May Stars are shown here and on the opposite page. Their positions are correct for May 7th at 11 p.m. and May 22nd at 10 p.m., and for four minutes earlier on each succeeding night, e.g. May 8th at 10.56 p.m., 9th at 10.52 p.m., 10th at 10.48 p.m., 23rd at 9.56 p.m., &c.

This aspect of the heavens is also correct for April 22nd at midnight.

The Stars move from the positions here shown to those on the next pair of Aspect Charts in the space of two hours.

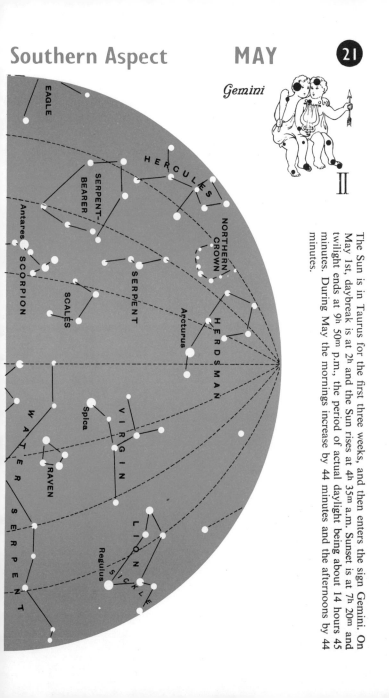

*Gemini*

♊

The Sun is in Taurus for the first three weeks, and then enters the sign Gemini. On May 1st, daybreak is at 2h and the Sun rises at 4h 35m a.m. Sunset is at 7h 20m and twilight ends at 9h 50m p.m., the period of actual daylight being about 14 hours 45 minutes. During May the mornings increase by 44 minutes and the afternoons by 44 minutes.

*Gemini*

II

The principal June Stars are shown here and on the opposite page. Their positions are correct for June 6th at 11 p.m. and June 22nd at 10 p.m., and for four minutes earlier on each succeeding night, e.g. June 7th at 10.56 p.m., 8th at 10.52 p.m., 9th at 10.48 p.m., 23rd at 9.56 p.m., &c.

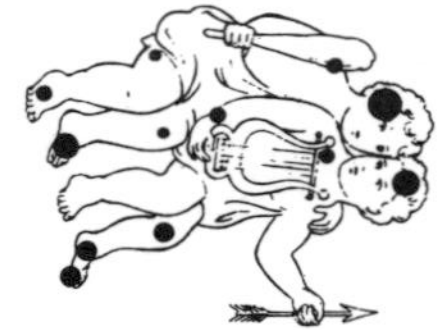

This aspect of the heavens is also correct for May 22nd at midnight.

The Stars move from the positions here shown to those on the next pair of Aspect Charts in the space of two hours.

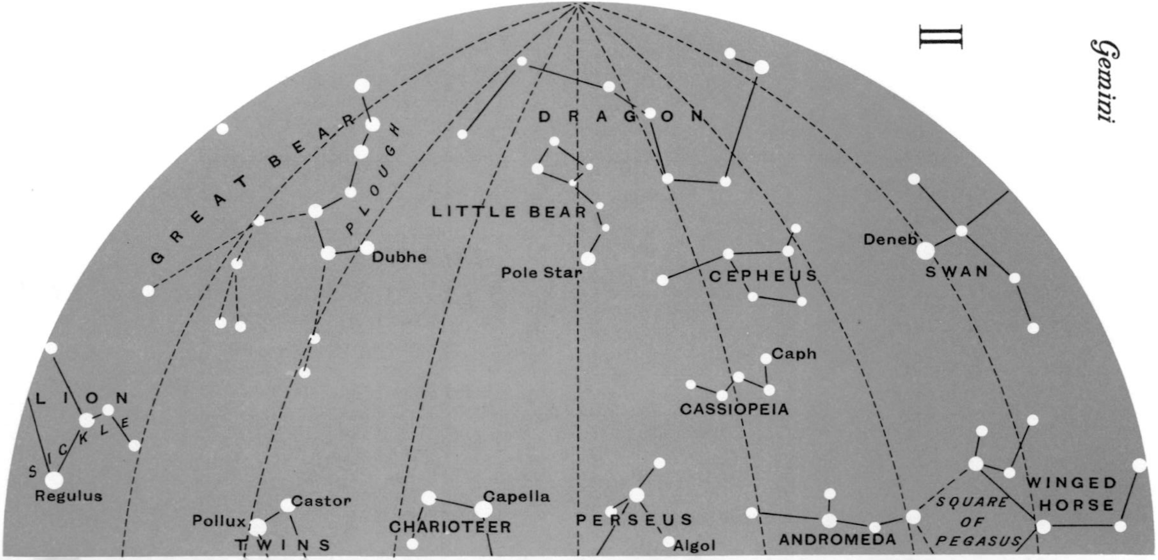

WINGED HORSE

SQUARE OF PEGASUS

Deneb

SWAN

ANDROMEDA

Caph

CEPHEUS

CASSIOPEIA

Algol

PERSEUS

DRAGON

Capella

LITTLE BEAR

Pole Star

CHARIOTEER

Dubhe

PLOUGH

Castor

TWINS

GREAT BEAR

Pollux

LION

SICKLE

Regulus

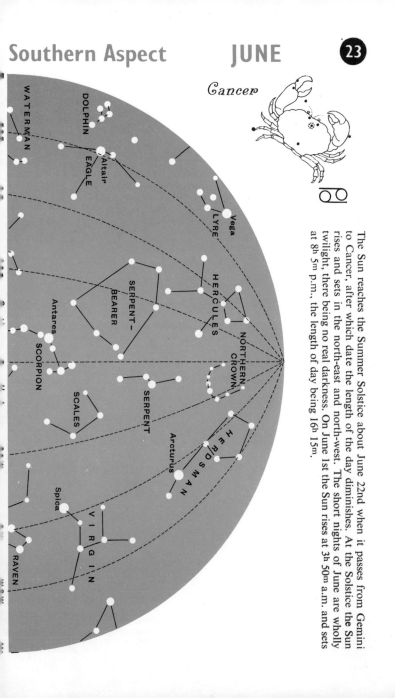

*Cancer*

The Sun reaches the Summer Solstice about June 22nd when it passes from Gemini to Cancer, after which date the length of the day diminishes. At the Solstice the Sun rises and sets in the north-east and north-west. The short nights of June are wholly twilight, there being no real darkness. On June 1st the Sun rises at 3h 50m a.m. and sets at 8h 5m p.m., the length of day being 16h 15m.

WATERMAN

DOLPHIN

EAGLE

Altair

LYRE

Vega

HERCULES

SERPENT-BEARER

Antares

SCORPION

NORTHERN CROWN

SCALES

SERPENT

Arcturus

HERDSMAN

Spica

VIRGIN

RAVEN

*Cancer*

The principal July Stars are shown here and on the opposite page. Their positions are correct for July 7 at 11 p.m. and July 22nd at 10 p.m., and for four minutes earlier on each succeeding night, e.g. July 8th at 10.56 p.m., 23rd at 9.56 p.m., 24th at 9.52 p.m., 25th at 9.48 p.m., &c.

This aspect of the heavens is also correct for June 22nd at midnight.

The Stars move from the positions here shown to those on the next pair of Aspect Charts in the space of two hours.

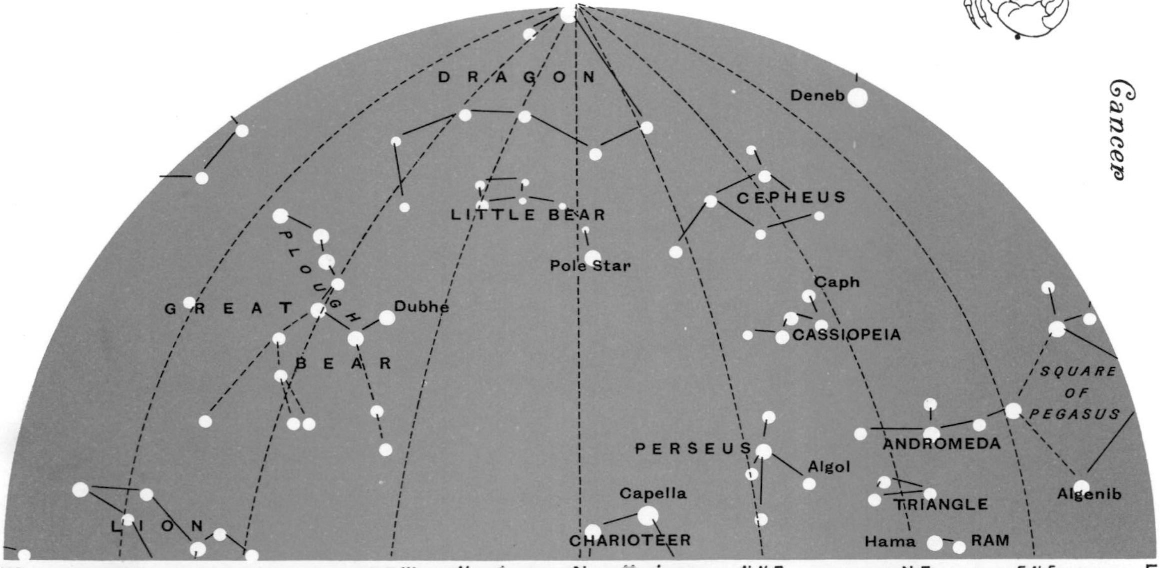

SQUARE OF PEGASUS — Algenib — ANDROMEDA — TRIANGLE — RAM — Hama — Deneb — CEPHEUS — Caph — CASSIOPEIA — Algol — PERSEUS — Capella — CHARIOTEER — Pole Star — LITTLE BEAR — DRAGON — Dubhe — PLOUGH — GREAT BEAR — LION

*Leo*

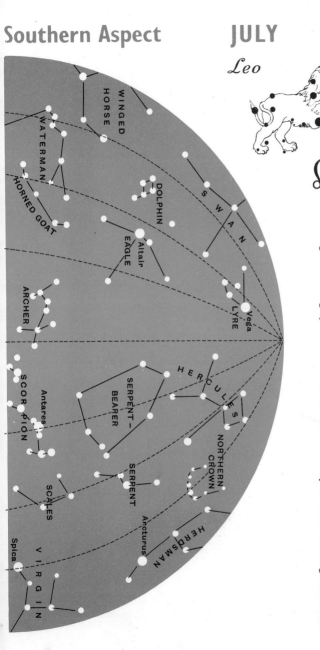

Until the Sun passes from Cancer into the sign Leo, about the 21st day, there is no real darkness. On July 1st sunrise is at 3h 50m a.m. and sunset at 8h 20m p.m., the length of day being 16 hours 30 minutes. The period of actual daylight now diminishes, the mornings decreasing by 34 minutes and the afternoons by 30 minutes during the month.

*Leo*

♌

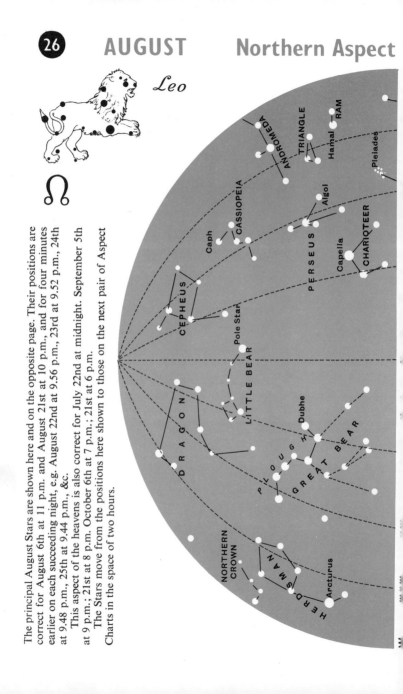

The principal August Stars are shown here and on the opposite page. Their positions are correct for August 6th at 11 p.m. and August 21st at 10 p.m., and for four minutes earlier on each succeeding night, e.g. August 22nd at 9.56 p.m., 23rd at 9.52 p.m., 24th at 9.48 p.m., 25th at 9.44 p.m., &c.

This aspect of the heavens is also correct for July 22nd at midnight. September 5th at 9 p.m.; 21st at 8 p.m. October 6th at 7 p.m.; 21st at 6 p.m.

The Stars move from the positions here shown to those on the next pair of Aspect Charts in the space of two hours.

TRIANGLE

RAM
Hamal

ANDROMEDA

Pleiades

CASSIOPEIA

Algol

Caph

PERSEUS

CHARIOTEER

Capella

CEPHEUS

Pole Star

LITTLE BEAR

DRAGON

Dubhe

PLOUGH

GREAT BEAR

NORTHERN CROWN

HERDSMAN

Arcturus

*Virgo*

♍

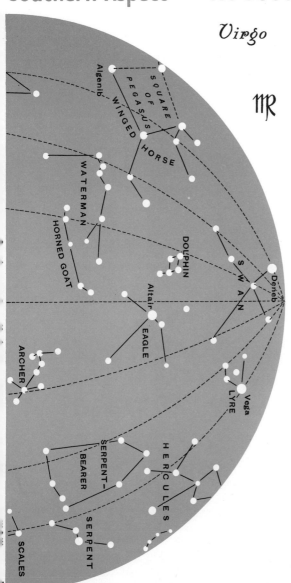

The Sun is in the sign Leo until August 21st, when it enters Virgo. On August 1st, day breaks at 1h 30m. and sunrise is at 4h 25m a.m. The Sun sets about 7h 45m and twilight ends at 10h 40m p.m. the length of actual daylight being 15 hours 20 minutes. During the month the mornings decrease by 47 minutes and the afternoons by 59 minutes.

*Virgo*

♍

The principal September Stars are shown here and on the opposite page. Their positions are correct for September 5th at 11 p.m. and September 21st at 10 p.m.; and for four minutes earlier on each succeeding night, e.g. September 1st at 11.16 p.m., 6th at 10.56 p.m., 22nd at 9.56 p.m., &c.

This aspect of the heavens is also correct for August 21st at midnight; October 6th at 9 p.m.; 21st at 8 p.m. November 5th at 7 p.m.; 21st at 6 p.m.

The Stars move from the positions here shown to those on the next pair of Aspect Charts in the space of two hours.

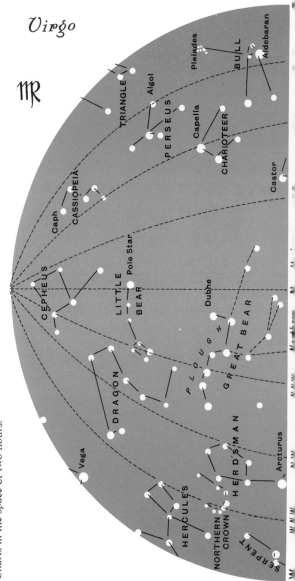

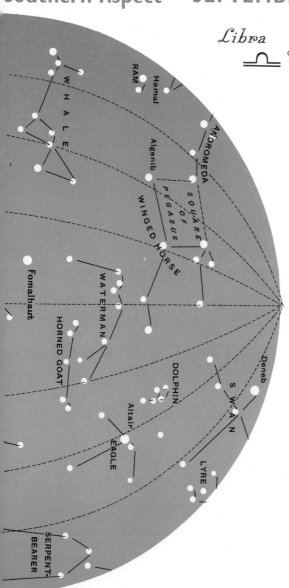

*Libra*

♎

The Autumnal Equinox occurs about September 22nd, when the Sun enters the sign of Libra, and day and night are equal all over the world. Autumn now begins. On September 1st daybreak is at 3h 5m and Sun rises at 5h 15m a.m. Sunset is at 6h 45m and twilight ends at 8h 50m p.m., the period of actual daylight being 13 hours 30 minutes. On September 22nd the Sun rises and sets due east and west. During the month the mornings decrease by 46 minutes and the afternoons by 66 minutes.

*Libra*

The principal October Stars are shown here and on the opposite page. Their positions are correct for October 6th at 11 p.m. and October 21st at 10 p.m., and for four minutes earlier on each succeeding night, e.g. October 1st at 11.20 p.m., 7th at 10.56 p.m., 22nd at 9.56 p.m., &c.

This aspect of the heavens is also correct for September 21st at midnight; November 5th at 9 p.m.; 21st at 8 p.m. December 6th at 7 p.m.; 21st at 6 p.m.

The Stars move from the positions here shown to those on the next pair of Aspect Charts in the space of two hours.

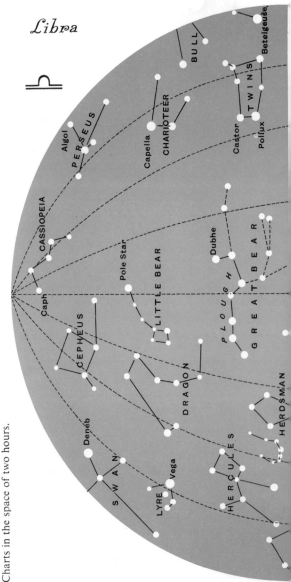

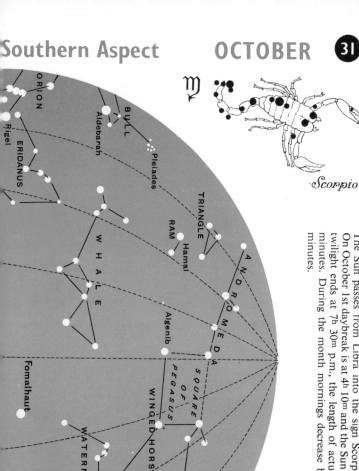

♏

*Scorpio*

The Sun passes from Libra into the sign Scorpio during the last week of October. On October 1st daybreak is at 4h 10m and the Sun rises at 6 a.m. Sunset is at 5h 38m and twilight ends at 7h 30m p.m., the length of actual daylight being about 11 hours 40 minutes. During the month mornings decrease by 51 minutes and afternoons by 64 minutes.

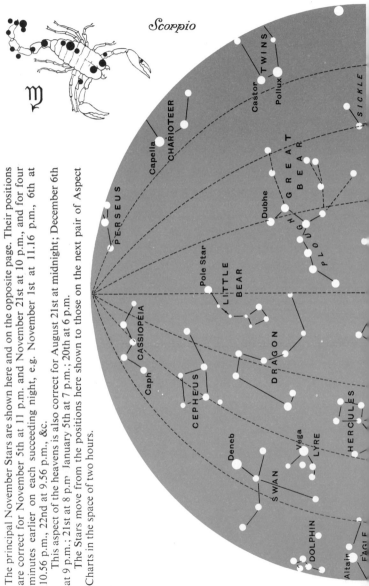

*Scorpio*

The principal November Stars are shown here and on the opposite page. Their positions are correct for November 5th at 11 p.m. and November 21st at 10 p.m., and for four minutes earlier on each succeeding night, e.g. November 1st at 11.16 p.m., 6th at 10.56 p.m., 22nd at 9.56 p.m., &c.

This aspect of the heavens is also correct for August 21st at midnight; December 6th at 9 p.m.; 21st at 8 p.m January 5th at 7 p.m.; 20th at 6 p.m.

The Stars move from the positions here shown to those on the next pair of Aspect Charts in the space of two hours.

## Sagittarius

The Sun passes from Scorpio into the sign of Sagittarius about November 24th. On November 1st, day breaks at 5h and sunrise is at 6h 55m a.m. The Sun sets at 4h 35m and twilight ends at 6h 25m p.m., the length of actual daylight being about 9 hours 40 minutes. During the month the mornings decrease by 49 minutes and the afternoons by 40 minutes.

Betelgeuse

ORION

HARE

Rigel

ERIDANUS

BULL

Aldebaran

Pleiades

PERSEUS

Algol

TRIANGLE

Hamal

RAM

WHALE

ANDROMEDA

Algenib

SQUARE OF PEGASUS

WINGED HORSE

WATERMAN

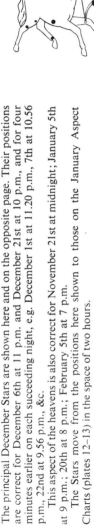

*Sagittarius*

The principal December Stars are shown here and on the opposite page. Their positions are correct for December 6th at 11 p.m. and December 21st at 10 p.m., and for four minutes earlier on each succeeding night, e.g. December 1st at 11.20 p.m., 7th at 10.56 p.m., 22nd at 9.56 p.m., &c.

This aspect of the heavens is also correct for November 21st at midnight; January 5th at 9 p.m.; 20th at 8 p.m.; February 5th at 7 p.m.

The Stars move from the positions here shown to those on the January Aspect Charts (plates 12–13) in the space of two hours.

Regulus

LION

SICKLE

GREAT BEAR

PLOUGH

Dubhe

Pole Star

LITTLE BEAR

DRAGON

PERSEUS

Vega

LYRE

CASSIOPEIA

CEPHEUS

Caph

SWAN

Deneb

WINGED HORSE

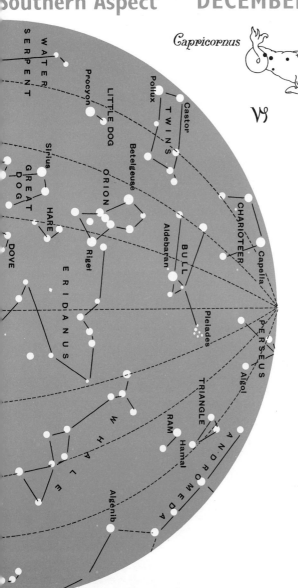

Capricornus

♑

The Sun reaches the Winter Solstice on December 22nd, when it passes from Sagittarius into the sign of Capricornus, after which the days begin to lengthen. At the Solstice the Sun rises and sets in the south-east and south-west. On December 1st, day breaks at 5h 40m and sunrise is at 7h 40m a.m. The Sun sets at 3h 55m and twilight ends at 5h 55m p.m. the length of daylight being about 8 hours 10 minutes. During the month the mornings decrease by 23 minutes and the afternoons increase by 5 minutes.

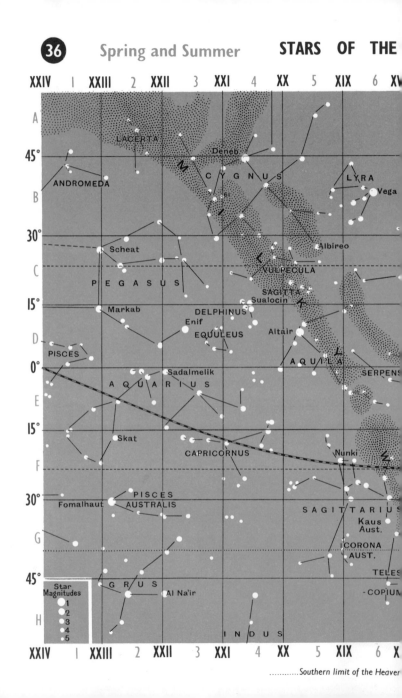

XXIV   I   XXIII   2   XXII   3   XXI   4   XX   5   XIX   6   X

A

45°

B

LACERTA

Deneb

C Y G N U S

61

LYRA

Vega

ANDROMEDA

30°

Scheat

Albireo

C

P E G A S U S

VULPECULA

SAGITTA

15°

Markab

Enif

DELPHINUS

Sualocin

EQUULEUS

Altair

D

A Q U I L A

PISCES

0°

SERPENS

Sadalmelik

A Q U A R I U S

E

15°

Skat

CAPRICORNUS

Nunki

F

30°

Fomalhaut

PISCES
AUSTRALIS

S A G I T T A R I U S

Kaus
Aust.

G

CORONA
AUST.

TELES

45°

COPIUM

Star
Magnitudes

1
2
3
4
5

G R U S

Al Na'ir

H

I N D U S

XXIV   I   XXIII   2   XXII   3   XXI   4   XX   5   XIX   6   X

............Southern limit of the Heaven

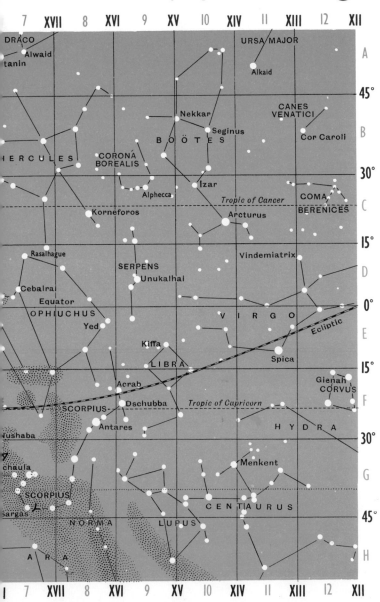

7  XVII  8  XVI  9  XV  10  XIV  11  XIII  12  XII

DRACO
Alwaid
tanin                                    URSA MAJOR                          A

                                              Alkaid                         45°

                         Nekkar              CANES
                              Seginus        VENATICI                        B
                    B O Ö T E S                 Cor Caroli
HERCULES        CORONA
                BOREALIS                                                     30°

                         Izar                                    COMA
              Alphecca                    Arcturus            BERENICES      C
        Korneforos                                                           
        Tropic of Cancer                                                     15°
Rasalhague                              Vindemiatrix                         D
                SERPENS
Cebalrai        Unukalhai                                                    
Equator                                                                      0°
OPHIUCHUS                        V I R G O
        Yed                                              Ecliptic            E
              Kiffa                                                          
                                                        Spica                15°
                L I B R A                                        Gienah
        Acrab                                                   CORVUS        F
        Dschubba        Tropic of Capricorn                                  
Nushaba         Antares                        H Y D R A                     30°

chaula                              Menkent                                  G
SCORPIUS
argas                        C E N T A U R U S                               45°
        N O R M A        L U P U S
A R A                                                                        H

7  XVII  8  XVI  9  XV  10  XIV  11  XIII  12  XII

sible from any part of the British Isles

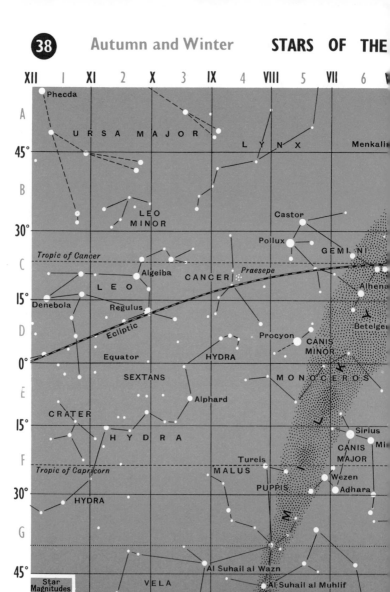

XII   1   XI   2   X   3   IX   4   VIII   5   VII   6

A

45°

B

30°

C

Tropic of Cancer

15°

D

0°

E

15°

F

Tropic of Capricorn

30°

G

45°

H

Phecda

URSA MAJOR

LYNX

Menkalina

LEO MINOR

Castor

Pollux

GEMINI

Algeiba   CANCER   Praesepe

Alhena

LEO

Denebola

Regulus

Betelge

Ecliptic

Procyon

CANIS MINOR

Equator

HYDRA

SEXTANS

MONOCEROS

Alphard

CRATER

HYDRA

Sirius

CANIS MAJOR

Mi

Tureis

Wezen

MALUS

Adhara

PUPPIS

HYDRA

Al Suhail al Wazn

VELA

Al Suhail al Muhlif

ARGO   NAVIS

Star Magnitudes
1
2
3
4
5

Markeb

CARINA

Canopus

XII   1   XI   2   X   3   IX   4   VIII   5   VII   6

..............Southern limit of the Heaven

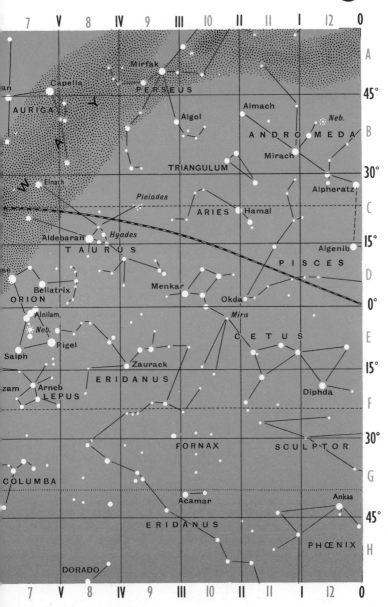

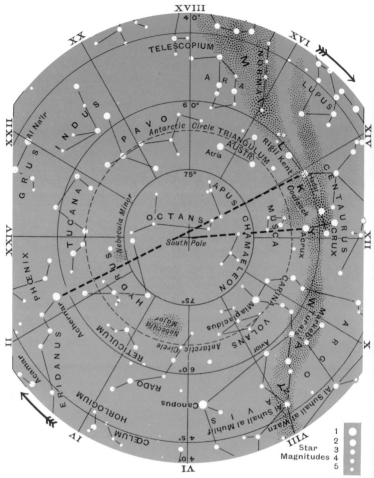

The Stars shown on this Plate comprise all Constellations which are *never visible* to the observer at the latitude of London. The stars indicating the position of the southern celestial pole are linked by a black pecked line; the pole is approximately half-way between Achernar and the north-south axis of the Southern Cross (Crux).

# Notes on the constellations and principal stars

The reference gives the page number of the Monthly Aspect Chart on which the constellation first appears, if any, and its direction, and of the detailed charts (pp. 9, 36–40), followed by the section. Numerals in brackets after the names of the stars indicate their magnitudes.

**ANDROMEDA** *12* WNW; *38–39* B 11
*Principal stars:* Alpheratz (2.1), Mirach (2), Almach (2).
Andromeda is immediately below Cassiopeia, in line with it and the Pole Star. It is most conspicuous in autumn and early winter, but is visible nearly all the year round. Alpheratz forms the upper left-hand corner of the Square of Pegasus. A remarkable nebula, visible to the naked eye in clear weather, is included in this star-group.

**APUS—The Bird of Paradise** *40*

**AQUARIUS—The Waterman or Water-bearer**. *23* ESE; *36–37* E 2
*Principal stars:* Sadalmelik (3), Skat (3).
An extensive constellation below Pegasus; contains no notable stars.

**AQUILA—The Eagle** *21* E; *36–37* D 5
*Principal star:* Altair (0.9)
Altair has a clear, bluish-white radiance, seen to best advantage in the evenings of early autumn, when the star is midway between the Zenith and the Horizon. It lies between two fairly bright stars, and forms with them a straight line, which, if produced across the Milky Way, leads to Vega. Altair, Vega (in Lyra) and Deneb (in Cygnus) form a great triangle worth memorizing as a guide to other groups. Altair is the apex of the triangle.

**ARA—The Altar** *36–37* H 7; *40*

**ARGO˙NAVIS—The Ship Argo** *38–39* H 3; *40*
*Principal stars:* Canopus (0.9), Miaplacidus (1.8), Al Suhail al Muhlif (1), Tureis (2), Markeb (2), Al Suhail al Wazn (2), Avior (2).
Most of this extensive constellation, including Canopus, the second brightest star in the heavens, is too far south to be visible from lat. 50°N.

PUPPIS (The Poop), CARINA (The Keel), MALUS (The Mast), and VELA (The Sails) are sub-divisions of this group.

**ARIES—The Ram** *13* W; *38–39* C 10
*Principal star:* Hamal (2.2).
Two insignificant groups of these stars may be seen in winter below Andromeda, on a line from Cassiopeia through Almach. The lower is ARIES and the upper TRIANGULUM, easily recognizable by its shape.

**AURIGA—The Charioteer**  *13* SW; *9*; *38–39* B.7
*Principal stars:* Capella (The Little Goat) (0.2), Menkalinan (2).
Auriga lies midway between Orion and the Pole Star, and is conse-
quently most conspicuous in winter, when it crosses the Meridian
near the Zenith in the wake of Cassiopeia. Capella is in line with
Megrez and Dubhe (Plough); it has an intense yellowish brilliance,
and never sets.

**BOÖTES—The Herdsman or Ox-driver**  *12* NE; *36–37* B 10
*Principal stars:* Arcturus (0.2), Nekkar (3), Seginus (3). The curve
of the "handle" of the Plough is continued by the stars of the right
side of Boötes, passes through Arcturus and terminates in Spica
(Virgo). Boötes is characteristic of the short summer nights, when
Arcturus, a bright reddish-yellow star, is the most striking object in
the southern aspect of the heavens, and the third brightest star in
the northern hemisphere.

**CAELUM—The Sculptor's Chisel**  *40*

**CANCER—The Crab**  *38–39* C 4
A group of inconspicuous stars between Regulus (Leo) and Pollux
(Gemini). It contains the famous cluster known as Praesepe, or the
Beehive.

**CANES VENATICI—The Greyhounds or Hunting Dogs**  *36–37* B 12
Cor Caroli (2) or Charles's Heart, the only noticeable star, was
so named because it is said to have been unusually bright when
Charles II re-entered London on his Restoration. It is situated in a
part of the sky, otherwise destitute of bright stars, between Virgo
and the "handle" of the Plough. There are known to be at least
30,000 stars in this cluster.

**CANIS MAJOR—The Great Dog**  *13* SSE; *38–39* F 6
*Principal stars:* Sirius (1.6), Mirzam (2), Adhara (1.6), Wezen (2).
Canis Major rises in the SE, sets in the SW, and reaches its greatest
altitude in mid-winter, when it is below and to the left of Orion.
Sirius, "the blazing Dog Star," shines with an intense greenish light
near the Southern Horizon during the winter months. It is the
brightest star of the heavens, and one of the nearest to the Earth.

**CANIS MINOR—The Little Dog**  *13* SE; *38–39* D 5
Canis Minor lies to the left of Orion and in line with Bellatrix and
Betelgeuse; being higher in the sky it is visible for a longer period
than Canis Major. Procyon (0.5) a pale yellow star, forms with
Sirius and Betelgeuse a great equilateral triangle which is one of the
most striking features of the southern sky in winter.

**CAPRICORNUS—The Horned Goat or Sea-Goat**  *25* SE; *36–37* F 3
Its position near the Horizon is indicated by the line of the three
bright stars in Aquila. The most westerly star of the group can be
resolved with the unaided eye into a pair, both of which have, in
fact, fainter companions.

**CARINA.** See Argo Navis.

**CASSIOPEIA** *12* NW; *9*
    *Principal stars:* Schedar (2.1 to 2.6), Caph (2).
This group resembles a distorted letter W drawn slantwise across the Milky Way on the opposite side of the Pole Star from the Plough. Cassiopeia is overhead in autumn and early winter, and being always visible and easily recognized is a useful guide to the location of less familiar star-groups.

**CENTAURUS—The Centaur** *36–37* G 10; *40*
    *Principal stars:* Rigil Kent (0.1), a navigation star, is the nearest star but one to the Earth, only four light years away. It is a double star, though the two cannot be distinguished by the naked eye. Hadar (0.9) and Menkent (3) are also navigation stars.

**CEPHEUS.** *12* NNW; *9*
Alderaimin (2) lies between Deneb (Cygnus) and the Pole Star.

**CETUS—The Whale or Sea-Monster** *29* SE; *38–39* E 11
    *Principal stars:* Diphda (2.2), Menkar (2), Mira (5).
Rises due E. and crosses the southern sky in advance of Orion, in the autumn. The only interesting feature is Mira, a star which varies from 3rd to 9th magnitude in the comparatively long period of 11 months, during half of which time it is invisible to the naked eye.

**CHAMÆLEON—Chameleon** *40*

**COLUMBA—Noah's Dove** *13* S; *38–39* G 7. See Lepus

**COMA BERENICES—Berenice's Hair** *36–37* C 12. See Virgo

**CORONA AUSTRALIS** or **COROLLA—The Southern Crown**
*36–37* G 6

**CORONA BOREALIS—The Northern Crown** *14* NE; *36–37* B 9
Alphecca (2.3) is the brightest of this semicircle of small stars, between Boötes and Hercules.

**CORVUS—The Crow or Raven** *17* SSE; *36–37* F 12
Gienah (2) and three other bright stars form a lozenge-shaped figure below Virgo. They must be sought low in the S. in spring. Six stars grouped to the right of Corvus represent CRATER.

**CRATER—The Cup** *38–39* E 1. See Corvus

**CRUX AUSTRALIS—The Southern Cross** *40*
    *Principal stars:* Acrux (1), Gacrux (2). See note on page 40.
Close to the Cross there is a gap in the Milky Way which is absolutely devoid of stars, and for this reason has been called the "Coalsack".

**CYGNUS—The Swan or Northern Cross**     *12* NNW, *36–37* B 4
   *Principal stars:* Deneb (1.3), Albireo (3).
Cygnus is a striking feature of the heavens during late summer and autumn when it passes directly overhead, and is recognizable as a great cross lying on the Milky Way, near Vega. Deneb is less brilliant than most first magnitude stars. The small star marked 61 on Plate 36–37 is one of the nearest stars to the Earth, visible from these latitudes. It is 64,800,000,000,000 miles away, the first stellar distance measured (1838).

**DELPHINUS—The Dolphin**     *20* ENE; *36–37* D 4
The Dolphin is a compact group of four stars forming a small lozenge, with a fifth below it, lying close to the Milky Way, and almost in line with the two lower stars of the Square of Pegasus. The figure cannot be mistaken when the sky is clear. EQUULEUS is a group of five fainter stars nearer to Pegasus.

**DORADO—The Sword Fish**     *38–39* H 8; *40*

**DRACO—The Dragon**     *12* N; *9*; *36–37* A 7
   *Principal stars:* Eltanin (Etamin) (2), Alwaid (3), Thuban (4).
Draco is a stream of fairly bright stars extending from close to Hercules up to the border of CEPHEUS, and thence curving back round URSA MINOR to a point between the Pole Star and the Pointers. Its brightest stars are grouped about a line drawn from Megrez (Plough) to Vega (Lyra).

**EQUULEUS—The Horse's Head**     *36–37* D 3. See Delphinus

**ERIDANUS—The River Eridanus or Po**     *31* ESE; *38–39* F 8
   *Principal stars:* Achernar (0.6), Cursa (3), Zaurack (3), Acamar (3).
Eridanus is a long winding stream of stars which begins close to the right of Rigel (Orion), flows west towards Cetus, and curving back thence is finally lost to sight below the Southern Horizon.

**FORNAX—The Furnace**     *38–39* G 10

**GEMINI—The Twins**     *13* SE; *38–39* C 5
   *Principal stars:* Pollux (1.2), Castor (1.6), Alhena (1.9).
Castor, a white star, and Pollux, with a golden tinge, represent the heads of the Twins at the eastern end of the constellation, which rises higher on the sky than Orion, in line with Betelgeuse and Rigel. In a telescope Castor resolves itself into three pairs of twin stars. Between the Twins and Polaris the sky is empty of bright stars.

**GRUS—The Crane**     *36–37* H 2; *40*
   *Principal star:* Al Na'ir (2).

**HERCULES**     *14* NE; *36–37* B 7
A summer constellation; the four brightest stars form an irregular quadrilateral to the left of Corona, on a line between Vega and Arcturus, and include an unusually red star.

**HORLOGIUM—The Clock**                                   *40*

**HYDRA—The Water-Serpent**                *13* ESE; *38–39* F 2
Alphard (The Solitary) (2.2) was so named on account of the dearth
of bright stars in its vicinity. Hydra extends from the compact group
of four stars just below Cancer to a star beneath Spica, and is the
largest constellation in the heavens.

**HYDRUS—The Water-Snake**                                *40*

**INDUS—The Indian**                              *36–37* H 4; *40*

**LACERTA—The Lizard**                               *36–37* A 2

**LEO—The Lion**                               *15* ESE; *38–39* C 2
  *Principal stars:* Regulus or Cor Leonis (1.3), Denebola (2.2),
  Algeiba (2).
Leo is typical of the night sky of spring, when Orion is settling in the
W, Megrez and Phecda (Plough) point to Regulus, the "Handle"
of the Sickle. The stars of the latter group closely resemble the form
assigned to them and are easily recognized. The remaining part of
Leo, shaped like a triangle, lies some distance to the left. A feature
of Leo is the meteoric shower occurring every November, when the
Leonids appear to issue from a point on the sky close to the Sickle.

**LEO MINOR—The Little Lion**                        *38–39* B 2

**LEPUS—The Hare**                              *13* S; *38–39* F 7
The small star-group immediately below the "feet" of Orion, south
of Lepus is COLUMBA, which is only seen for a brief period in
winter.

**LIBRA—The Balance or Scales**                *19* SE; *36–37* E 9
  *Principal star:* Zuben'ubi (3).
Visible in summer, low on the sky beneath Arcturus.

**LUPUS—The Wolf**                                   *36–37* H 9

**LYNX—The Lynx**                                   *9*; *38–39* A 4

**LYRA—The Lyre**                      16 NE; *9*; *36–37* B 6
  *Principal stars:* Vega (0.1), Sulaphat (3).
Vega is a brilliant bluish-white star prominent near the Zenith on
summer nights, when Capella is low in the N. The Pole Star is about
halfway between Vega and Capella, the three making a great hori-
zontal line across the heavens in autumn and spring. VEGA dips
below the northern horizon of an observer in the extreme south
of Britain, but elsewhere it is a true circumpolar star and never sets.
With Altair and Deneb it forms a conspicuous V, with Vega at the
top of the right leg of the V. See note on Altair in Aquila.

**MALUS.** See Argo Navis.

**MONOCEROS—The Unicorn**                            *38–39* E 5
A minor constellation extending across the Milky Way east of Orion.

**MUSCA AUSTRALIS—The Southern Fly**                      *40*

**NORMA—The Square** *36–37* H 8; *40*

**OCTANS—The Octant** *40*
This constellation includes the South Celestial Pole.

**OPHIUCHUS—The Serpent-holder or Serpent-Bearer** *19* ESE
*36–37* E 7
*Principal stars:* Rasalhague (2.1), Cebalrai (2), Yed (3).
Ophiuchus is the widespread star group immediately below Hercules.
Barnard's "Proper Motion Star" in this constellation is the nearest
known star to the Earth. SERPENS can be traced from below
Corona across the Serpent-Bearer and into the Milky Way beside
Aquila.

**ORION—The Hunter** *13* S; *38–39* D 7
*Principal stars:* Betelgeuse (0.1 to 1.2), Rigel (0.3), Bellatrix (1.7),
Alnitak (2.0), Saiph (2).
Orion, the most brilliant star-group of all, and the chief guide to the
stars of the southern aspect of the heavens, rises and sets due E and
W. The straight line of the three bright stars in Orion's "belt," if
produced to the right (north-west) leads to Aldebaran (Taurus), if
extended an equal distance to the left (north-east) it reaches Sirius
(Canis Major). Betelgeuse varies considerably in brilliance and has a
reddish tinge, visibly contrasting with the hard white radiance of
Rigel. Keen sight can detect the Great Nebula in Orion as a haze of
light round the middle star of the "sword" which hangs from the
Hunter's belt.

**PAVO—The Peacock** *40*
*Principal star:* Peacock (2).

**PEGASUS—The Winged Horse** *22* ENE; *36–37* C 2
*Principal stars:* Algenib (2), Markab (2), Scheat (2), Enif (2).
The Great Square of Pegasus, a quadrilateral of four bright stars
(Algenib, Markab and Scheat, with Alpheratz of Andromeda), is a
striking feature of the skies of late summer, autumn and early winter,
and is a most useful guide to less conspicuous constellations at these
seasons. When ascending the E sky, and again when descending
towards the NW, the "Square" becomes a broad diamond-shaped
figure, but it is unmistakable at all times. Pegasus crosses the meridian
in autumn somewhat higher on the sky than Orion at its culmination
in midwinter. A line drawn from Algenib to Polaris (through
Alpheratz in Andromeda and Caph in Cassiopeia) would roughly
indicate the Zero meridian from which Right Ascension is calculated.

**PERSEUS** *12* WNW; *9*; *38–39* A9
Mirfak (1.9) is the brightest star, and Algol (2) is a well-known
variable star which changes from 2nd to 4th magnitude in less than
three days. Perseus is a festoon of stars on the Milky Way, between
Capella and Cassiopeia.

**PHŒNIX.** 38–39 H 12; 40
*Principal star:* Ankaa (Nair al Zaurak) (2).

**PISCES—The Fishes** 38–39 D 11
*Principal star:* Okda (4).
A line of stars extending from Aquarius below the Square of Pegasus to Aries.

**PISCIS AUSTRALIS—The Southern Fish** 29 S; 36–37 F 2
Fomalhaut (1.3), the one bright star, is visible for a short time in autumn when the Horizon is clear. It should then be looked for in the S, below Aquarius, and in line with Scheat and Markab, the right-hand side of the Square of Pegasus.

**PUPPIS.** See Argo Navis.

**RETICULUM—The Net** 40

**SAGITTA—The Arrow** 36–37 C 4
Consists of four inconspicuous stars on the Milky Way above Aquila. Higher still, between Sagitta and Cygnus, a scattered group of small stars marks the position of VULPECULA.

**SAGITTARIUS—The Archer** 25 S; 36–37 G 5
*Principal stars:* Kaus Australis (1.9), Nunki (2), Nushaba (3).
Visible in summer near the S. Horizon, below Aquila. Somewhere in this group is generally considered by astronomers to be the real centre of the universe.

**SCORPIUS—The Scorpion** 21 SSE; 36–37 F 8
*Principal stars:* Antares (1.2), Dschubba (2), Acrab (2), Shaula (2).
A summer constellation, seen as a festoon of bright stars just above the Horizon, below Ophiuchus and the Serpent. Antares, the brightest star, has a reddish light, and is the largest star yet measured. During the short, light nights of June it is due S about midnight.

**SCULPTOR—Sculptor's Tools** 38–39 G 12

**SERPENS—The Serpent** 19 ESE; 36–37 D 9
*Principal star:* Unuk (2). See Ophiuchus.

**SEXTANS—The Sextant** 38–39 E 2

**TAURUS—The Bull** 13 SW; 38–39 D 8
*Principal stars:* Aldebaran (1.1), Elnath (1.8), Alcyone (2).
Elnath is midway between Capella (Auriga) and Betelgeuse (Orion). Aldebaran, a brilliant red star, lies considerably to the right of this line in the direction marked by the "belt" of Orion. It forms with four smaller stars the cluster known as Hyades. Higher on the right are the Pleiades. This well-known cluster has six stars easily visible to the naked eye, the brightest being Alcyone. The Pleiades first appear as a compact scintillating group.in the NE on the dark nights following the Harvest Moon, while the Hyades are yet below the Horizon.

**TELESCOPIUM—The Telescope** 36–37 G 6; 40

**TRIANGULUM—The Triangle**        *12* W; *38–39* B 10. See Aries
   *Principal star:* Atria (2).

**TRIANGULUM AUSTRALIS—The Southern Triangle**        *40*

**TUCANA—Tucan**        *40*

**URSA MAJOR—The Great Bear**        *12* NE; *9*
   *Principal stars.* Dubhe (1.9), Merak (2), Phecda (2), Megrez (3),
   Alioth (1.7), Mizar (2), Alkaid (Benetnasch) (1.9).

These seven stars form the Plough (also known as Charles's Wain
and the Dipper), which is the most conspicuous and familiar star-
group of the Northern Heavens. A line drawn through Merak and
Dubhe, the "Pointers", passes close to the Pole Star. Alkaid, the
tail star of the Plough handle, is a useful pointer to Arcturus to the
southward.

The Plough never sets, and is always high enough on the sky to
be easily seen; it is therefore the most useful guide to the location
of the North Celestial Pole. In winter the Plough is in the NE, with
the Pointers uppermost. During March and April it passes close to
the Zenith, and descending in the NW as summer advances, reaches
a position between the Pole Star and N. Horizon in the evenings of
October and November. An interesting feature of the group is the
small star Alcor, a companion of Mizar, visible to keen sight on a
clear night. Its position above one of the "horses" of Charles's Wain
has given it the popular name of the "Rider".

**URSA MINOR—The Little Bear**        *12* N; *9*
   *Principal stars:* Polaris (The Pole Star) (2.1), Kochab (2).

The Pole Star is so close to the North Celestial Pole that its own
revolution is negligible and it is accepted as indicating at all times
the true N. It is thus the most important guide-star of the heavens.
The Little Bear is otherwise an inconspicuous group, and can be
traced as a faint string of stars between Polaris and Kochab, with a
small rectangle at the latter end. The line Polaris—Kochab points
to Boötes.

**VELA. See Argo Navis.**

**VIRGO—The Virgin**        *15* ESE; *36–37* E 11
   *Principal stars:* Spica (1.2), Vindemiatrix (2).

Virgo is characteristic of the nights of early spring, and crosses the
meridian in March. Spica lies at the end of the curve of the "handle"
of the Plough, continued through Arcturus. Spica and Arcturus with
Denebola form a nearly equilateral triangle. A line through Spica
and Vindemiatrix to the Plough crosses a portion of the sky deficient
in bright stars, Cor Caroli (Canes Venatici) is the only prominent
star near this line and between it and Vindemiatrix is a group of
very faint stars known as COMA BERENICES.

**VOLANS —The Flying Fish**        *40*

**VULPECULA—The Fox and Goose**        *36–37* C 4. See Sagitta.

# The Chief Features of the Moon

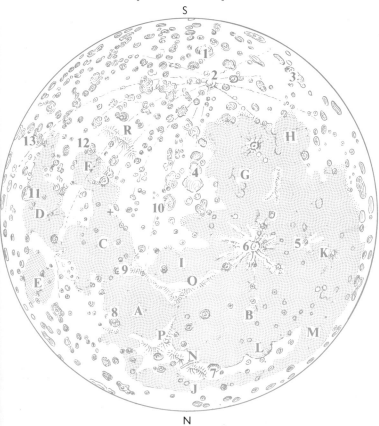

S

N

## Plains or Ocean Beds and Mountains

| | | |
|---|---|---|
| A | Mare Serenitatis | G Mare Nubium |
| B | ,, Imbrium | H ,, Humorum |
| C | ,, Tranquilitatis | I ,, Vaporum |
| D | ,, Fecunditatis | J ,, Frigoris |
| E | ,, Crisium | K Oceanus Procellarum |
| F | ,, Nectaris | L Sinus Iridum |

M Sinus Roris
N The Alps
O The Apennine Mts.
P The Caucasus Mts.
R The Altai Mts.

## Principal Craters

| | | |
|---|---|---|
| 1 Clavius | 5 Kepler | 10 Hipparchus |
| 2 Tycho | 6 Copernicus | 11 Langrenus |
| 3 Schickard | 7 Plato | 12 Fracastorius |
| 4 Alphonsus | 8 Posidonius | 13 Petavius |
| | 9 Plinius | |

+ Apollo 11 Landing Site

# The Far Side of the Moon

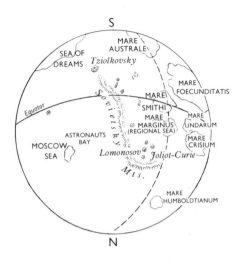

# Distances from the earth to the other planets

Distances given at nearest approach of planets to the earth.

| Name | Distance (1,000's miles) |
|---|---|
| VENUS | 26,000 |
| MARS | 34,600 |
| MERCURY | 49,505 |
| JUPITER | 350,000 |
| SATURN | 800,000 |
| URANUS | 1,700,000 |
| NEPTUNE | 2,700,000 |
| *PLUTO | 3,580,000 |

*Because of the extreme variation of distance between Pluto and the Sun it is not possible to give a figure strictly comparable with those of the other planets. The distance given is based on the mean distance of Pluto from the Sun.

NORTHERN HALF OF COMPASS CARD

To be used in conjunction with the Northern Aspect Charts. For instructions, see page 5.